CAIRO TRAFFIC

PHOENIX **POETS**

A SERIES EDITED BY ALAN SHAPIRO

Cairo Traffic

LLOYD SCHWARTZ

THE UNIVERSITY OF CHICAGO PRESS
Chicago and London

Lloyd Schwartz is the Frederick S. Troy Professor of English and co-director of the Creative Writing Program at the University of Massachusetts Boston, classical music editor of the *Boston Phoenix*, and a regular commentator on music and the arts on National Public Radio's *Fresh Air*. He is the author of two previous books of poems, *These People* and *Goodnight, Gracie*, and co-editor of *Elizabeth Bishop and Her Art*. He was awarded the 1994 Pulitzer Prize for criticism.

Title page and part-title page illustrations: Ralph Hamilton, *Ancient Egyptian Star Homunculus*, pencil on tracing paper, 1999.

The University of Chicago Press, Chicago 60637
The University of Chicago Press, Ltd., London
© 2000 by The University of Chicago
All rights reserved. Published 2000
Printed in the United States of America

09 08 07 06 05 04 03 02 01 00   1 2 3 4 5

ISBN: 0-226-74192-3 (cloth)
ISBN: 0-226-74193-1 (paper)

Library of Congress Cataloging-in-Publication Data
Schwartz, Lloyd, 1941–
    Cairo traffic / Lloyd Schwartz.
       p. cm. — (Phoenix poets)
    ISBN 0-226-74192-3 (cloth : alk. paper) — ISBN 0-226-74193-1 (paper : alk. paper)
    I. Title. II. Series.

PS3569.C5667 C35 2000
811'.54—dc21   99-048502

♾ The paper used in this publication meets the minimum requirements of the American National Standard for Information Sciences—Permanence of Paper for Printed Library Materials, ANSI Z39.48-1992

For Ralph Hamilton

Contents

Acknowledgments

The author gratefully acknowledges the editors and publishers of the following periodicals, in which these poems first appeared:

Agni: "Cairo Traffic"
Boulevard: "The Two Churches (A Dream)," "The Dream During My
      Mother's Recuperation"
The Cortland Review (Cortlandreview.com): "Sons," "Family Scene,"
      "Flutes," "The Condor Passes," "Brazilian Winter."
Harvard Magazine: "Renato's Dream"
Harvard Review: "Friendly Song"
The New Yorker: "Nostalgia (The Lake at Night)"
Orion: "Mist," "Father" (Winter 1998)
The Paris Review: "Proverbs from Purgatory," "Pornography"
Ploughshares: "No Orpheus" (vol. 23, no. 4)
Poetry: "Song"
Slate (www.slate.com): "The Two Horses (A Memory)," "He Tells His
      Mother What He's Working On," "Her Waltz." Reprinted with
      permission. Slate is a trademark of Microsoft Corporation.
      © 1999.
Tikkun: "She Forgets"

"Pornography" was selected for *The Best American Poetry 1994;* "She
Forgets," "The Two Horses (A Memory)," and "The Dream During My
Mother's Recuperation" were first broadcast on NPR's *Fresh Air;* "A True

Poem" and "He Tells His Mother What He's Working On" are included on the CD *One Side of the River* (Say That! Productions).

Special thanks to Gail Mazur, Michael McDowell, and Robert Polito for their contributions to "Proverbs from Purgatory"; to Regina Przybycien for her help with my Portuguese; to Renato Rezende; to David Stang; and to Frank Bidart, for his unflagging support and advice.

Grants from the National Endowment for the Arts and the United States Information Agency contributed invaluably to the composition of this book. "No Orpheus" was commissioned by the Cambridge Symphony Orchestra with funds from the Massachusetts Cultural Council.

A True Poem

I'm working on a poem that's so true, I can't show it to anyone.

I could never show it to anyone.

Because it says exactly what I think, and what I think scares me.

Sometimes it pleases me.

Usually it brings misery.

And this poem says exactly what I think.

What I think of myself, what I think of my friends, what I think about my lover.

Exactly.

Parts of it might please them, some of it might scare them.

Some of it might bring misery.

And I don't want to hurt them, I don't want to hurt them.

I don't want to hurt anybody.

I want everyone to love me.

Still, I keep working on it.

Why?

Why do I keep working on it?

Nobody will ever see it.

Nobody will ever see it.

I keep working on it even though I can never show it to anybody.

I keep working on it even though someone might get hurt.

Friendly Song
("Cançao Amiga")*

by Carlos Drummond de Andrade

I'm working on a song
in which my own mother sees her image,
everyone's mother sees her image,
and it speaks, it speaks just like two eyes.

I'm traveling along a roadway
that winds through many countries.
My old friends—if they don't see me,
I see them, I see and salute them.

I am giving away a secret
like someone who loves, or smiles.
In the most natural way
two caresses reach each other.

My whole life, all of our lives
make up a single diamond.
I've learned a few new phrases—
and to make others better.

I'm working on a song
that wakes men up
and lets children sleep.

*Printed on the Brazilian 50-cruzados note.

*

She Forgets

The one who told me about the Holocaust, who taught me moral distinctions, who gave me music and told me jokes, is in a nursing home: lonely, scared, surrounded only by people so much worse off (inarticulate, incapacitated, drooling), she thinks she's in a crazy house.

She's not crazy.

She's there—I put her there—because she can't take care of herself, can't be left alone.

She's old.

She forgets.

She forgets her medicine.

She forgets what she's not supposed to eat.

She forgets what day it is.

She remembers who she is—and who she was—and knows she's not herself.

She can't remember what's wrong with her ("What's wrong with me, honey?") or why she's there, but she knows her brain isn't working right.

Her brain needs air.

Oxygen has a hard time squeezing through her hardened arteries.

So her blood congeals.

Little clots cause little strokes, which destroy her memory.

Aspirin, which thins the blood and helps keep the oxygen flowing, might help her remember.

But she's old.

Part of her stomach has turned upside down.

Her food gets stuck in her chest, blocks her breath.

She panics, forces herself to vomit, which makes her bleed—which damages her heart.

A simple operation could fix her stomach.

But doctors won't operate on someone with a damaged heart.

And aspirin makes her bleed.

So she can't take aspirin.

So she forgets.

I live in another city.

Once, after I came to visit, she wasn't thinking about her food.

She ate too much, or too fast, and the food wouldn't go down.

So she panicked, forced herself to vomit, and had a heart attack.

She was in the hospital for three weeks (which she doesn't remember).

So I've had to put the one who gave me music and told me jokes, who taught me moral distinctions, and warned me never to forget the Holocaust—I've had to put her in a nursing home, a crazy house, where she's scared and lonely; where she stares out the window and asks: *"What day is today?"*

"Why can't I go home?"

"What's wrong with me, honey?"

"Why am I here?"

The Two Horses (A Memory)

You said you had lunch in Pittsfield, was it on North Street?

That reminds me of when we lived on the farm.

It must be eighty years ago.

We went to a one-room schoolhouse, didn't you drive past it once?

Each row was a different grade.

I sat in the first seat of the first row.

The teacher's name was Miss Brown.

She was so pretty.

I wonder if she's still alive.

The day before we left the farm our cat disappeared.

We couldn't find her anywhere.

I was sad for weeks.

Three months later she showed up at our new house in Pittsfield.

Robbins Avenue.

I can't think of the number now.

My sister was in New York.

She didn't like the people she was living with so she'd visit us.

She fell in love with the young man who lived next door.

Maurice.

Your uncle Maurice.

They got married and moved to Cleveland.

They're both gone now, aren't they?

You know, I can't picture her.

A few years later we moved to New York.

This just jumped into my mind: I must have been three years old.

We were still in Russia.

Mir.

A small town, but famous for its yeshiva.

My oldest brother—Joe—took our horses down to the river.

They were the two best horses in the town.

My father had a phaeton.

A beautiful old buggy.

He was like a taxi driver, he took people to Minsk.

Or Vilna.

That day he was at the station.

The passenger station, waiting for customers.

My brother was still just a kid.

He must have been washing the horses in the river.

I can remember—it was a hot day.

Maybe he was giving them a drink.

And while I was watching the reins got caught around a pole in the river.

The horses kept twisting the reins around that pole.

It was slippery, the reins kept sliding down under the water and they were pulling the horses down with them.

I ran into town and got my father who came running back with a knife in his teeth.

He jumped into the river with all his clothes on.

He took the knife and sawed away at the reins until he finally cut through.

He saved the horses.

I haven't thought about this in a thousand years.

It's like a dream: you get up it's forgotten.

Then it all comes back.

Didn't I ever tell you?

Look at me, I'm starting to cry.

What's there to cry about?

Such an old, old memory, why should it make me cry?

He Tells His Mother What He's Working On

I'm writing a poem about you.

> *You are? What's it about?*

It's the story about your childhood, the horses in the river.

> *The ones that nearly drowned? . . . I saved them.*

You told it to me just a few weeks ago.

> *I should dig up more of my memories.*

I wish you would.

> *Like when I lived on the farm and one of the girls fell down the well?*

Yes.

> *I forget if it was Rose or Pauline—it was a deep well.*

I remember that story.

> *Have you finished your poem?*

I'm still working on it.

You mean you're correcting it, with commas and semi-colons?

Exactly.

When can I see it?

As soon as it's finished.

Is it an epic?

It's not that long.

No, I mean all my thoughts, the flashes of what's going through my life, the whole family history . . . living through the woe, the river and the water.

I know.

Will it be published?

I have to finish it first.

It's better to write about real life, that's more important than writing something fanciful.

I try to write all my poems about real life.

You see, the apple never falls far from the tree.

I guess not.

You're my apple.

There's probably a worm crawling through that apple.

Then it's got something sweet to chew on.

Well, you're my tree.

Yes, I'm your tree—you're an apple, I'm a tree.

From *Brazilian Winter*

by Rogério Zola Santiago

Mist

Texture of silence—dry and clear—
then from the garage a sudden squeal
interrupts the TV twilight
to announce, beyond the *sucupira* door,
the arrival of the father, who enters, sits down
at the table with the lamp, and opens a book.
Memory contrasts his white hair,
almost silver, with the gold ring on his right hand
which he runs through it.
I lift my arm to touch
but stop at the violets and lilies in the window boxes.
In the corner of my eye,
rosary crystals spill and roll over the opaque blue
and aquamarine tiles on the floor of our colonial porch.
Grasshopper verities, humming lullabies . . .
An office of portraits
covered by a thickening varnish
of respect and distance.
A kitchen smell threads toward the birdhouse stage-set.
I bend over his table, holding within me my father
and anticipating my children—an unintelligible look
imprints itself on the pages of his book,

like a jet of sand in stained glass.
Graying ruins. Smoke.
In the foreground, a strong arm
tries to close the drawbridge-drawer
of my first dwelling.
Texture of blueberry bush, pomegranate, and raisins.
Where the "Good-to-see-you" bird whistles jokes
in the pleasant aftermath, and late bells ricochet.

Father

I keep recycling the father
from the grain planted in the ground,
irrigated and fertilized with nitrates from Chile,
the root, the seed, making its way from the Andes
into the ploughed earth.

I recycle the father
whose seed is planted in my flesh,
I become him in the crops
brought over on the caravelles,
in the red pouch of the frigate-pelican.

The father of cycles
puts dust into the ground,
and the Earth turns herself around
in the heat of resurrected desire—

then the father of centuries rests
under what he's planted.

Sons

My mother listens to the cries of one
and then the other (the ones she wants to spoil
with her body, with her skin), and my
own cries. Entering this labyrinth, she
puts back into the tree the spineless colors
of bankrupt Christmases. Our cries ricochet
from the veranda to the street, and
we all feel sorry for ourselves, except
for father, who's gone shopping and
is out buying slates. My mother
doesn't realize just how much she's succeeded in keeping
us from dying young. Yet ungrateful
and precipitous, we continue to demand that
she mend our socks.

Family Scene

They are like a fence
at the end of the afternoon—
a fat woman and
a tall man—
holding each other up,
while the children
eye a dog mounting his bitch.

At the Sacred Lagoon there are
family scenes
in the solitary depths of those
waters contaminated by time
that would pass almost unnoticed—were it
not for that howling.

Flutes

My stomach is stuffed from eating up
the view. Peruvian women
show me cornfields and hairy
pigs. The horses are dots of color
as I dive dizzily
into the meadows. Infinity
eats rats. In the Pisac Church
the natives and their buttocks under
the rain—their clothes: sadness and cold.

A sad people
in the solicitude of flutes
their bodies renouncing the coca leaves'
tea of wisdom before the calm siesta—

Laugh at yourself,
breathless tourist.

The Condor Passes

Magda dances with me.
Solange dances with me.
The condor laments. The panpipes go mute. No breath.
My face and hair hit the sun
in the alchemy of lies & truth.
Dance with me, History—melancholy/
ecstatic intercourse between memory
and a weathervane.

Brazilian Winter

Nadja wants to die.
She'll never find
her father (who's already dead) in
the body of a nonexistent lover.
She sobs and pushes me away,
then sobs and begs *"Don't go—*
don't go." Hair-on-Fire, Golden-Fur,
she blindly follows each morning—
the same lost morning she's detached
from Day and Night—
drifting numbly across the panorama
of unfinished power plants.
Nadja wants to—yet
she won't. She has yet to plunge
into the Brazilian winter, the one
without snow, so hot
it both melts and cools
her burning need to submit.

Translated with the author

Shut-Eye

He dreams he's shooting himself in the eye his left eye the barrel right up
against the eye he wants to blast open his eye *his eyes* shut tight stuck can't get
them to open the dark *(how dark?)* so dark he can't he can't breathe the steel
cold against his eyelid he angles it angles it up under his eyelid wedging it
wedging it up under his heart pounding under his eyelids one bullet could tear
apart the barrel heavy against his trembling finger squeezing the trigger his
heart pounding the dark so dark he's he's his heart pounding his suffocating
his trembling finger squeezing the trigger till he almost hears the shot that
opens that blasts open his eye *his eyes*

The Two Churches (A Dream)

"In the main square, there are two churches, not just one—two
    great Baroque churches, facing each other—decaying,
    yet magnificent. Almost identical, except that one
    is locked, and the door to the other is wide open.

    Early morning, not a cloud in the sky. I'm waiting outside.

    In the center of the square there's a monument,
    an obelisk. Like the 'hand' on a sundial, it casts a

long, narrow shadow.

It's already quite warm. I look in through the open door,
    peer in: it seems cool and dark inside. But I
    step back, as if I were waiting for someone to arrive.

    But that's impossible—I don't know anyone
    in this town. I can't even speak the language.

A man appears in the doorway—a round,
    ugly little man, with a face like a rubber ball.
    His hair is thin and greasy, his clothes disheveled.

    He has on a white shirt, but it's not tucked in,
    and not recently laundered.

                                His paunch
        hangs over his belt. He wears his pants low,
        to make room for his sagging stomach.

        He signals me to come inside.

I don't move. I seem to be staring into the sun.

He comes outside—smiles at me. He's missing
                several front teeth.
                                Fat, ugly, dirty—
        yet there's a sweetness, something almost
        cherubic about him. He touches me.
                                        He touches
        my shoulder and points inside. Then he nudges me, nudges

        my shoulder, and ushers me into the church.

It isn't dark at all. The light comes
                pouring in. There's no one else inside.

        He guides me around the rim of the nave. Each chapel
        is like a wedding cake, with a
        martyred saint in ecstasy on the top.

With his chubby fingers, he points out
                little details: the pockmark on one saint's face,
        a drop of blood on a bony hand, a crooked
        finger, a fingernail.
                        I'm struck by the
        shafts of light coming in through unseen openings.

        Each time he points, he touches me—nudges me

with the back of his hand, taps my shoulder, my
arm, my hip.

He leads me up to the foot of the altar: the body of Jesus
lying in an open sepulcher.
The little man
stands in front of me, looking into the sepulcher;
he swings his arm back, and the back of his hand

accidentally brushes across the front of my pants . . .

He turns and grins. Is he grinning
at me, or am I just imagining?

He leads me into a side chapel. The window is open,
but barred. On top of the wedding cake is the Blessed
Virgin. The little round man stands beside me.

He points to the Virgin, then swings back his arm until
the back of his hand touches my chest, presses my chest,

then slides down, below my waist, and brushes
across the front of my pants, presses
against the front of my pants.

There's no mistake: he's grinning at me, and his
gap-toothed grin

is a smile of sexual longing.

I don't move. I don't move
away. I let him press the back of his hand
against my pants—against what is growing in my pants.

Suddenly, he drops down on his knees and elbows, like a fat
         puppy—his elbows on the wooden floor,
         his fat rump sticking up into the air. He jiggles his pelvis
         up and down. He turns his head to look

         up at me. He's still grinning, his eyes
         are moist and glistening . . .

         I come around behind him. I bend over him,
         against him, against his fat behind. I wrap my arms
         around his round stomach.

Then we stand up. He unzips his pants and reaches his hand
         inside. I unzip my pants and reach my hand inside.

         He grins. He takes his hand out, looks
         up at the Virgin, and shakes his finger at me:

         'No, no. Not in church.' He grins from ear to

         pudgy ear. He's like one of the mischievous,
         plump-cheeked cherubs over the altar,
         blowing into a trumpet.

I come to him, put my arms around him, *embrace* him. He
         puts his arms around me—his mouth is wet; his lips
         are wet; his tongue is thick and wet.

         There's no one in the church.

         The light is pouring in.

He pushes me by the shoulder into the next chapel: St. Francis—
         with moist red lips, flushed, looking down at us
         with large, sad, yearning eyes:

                    Carved,
    the little man tells me, by the great saint-maker
    of that town—a cripple, who carved his statues
    with a knife strapped to his wrist . . .

    I understand every word—although the language is
    still obscure.

    I can't answer, I only nod.

His eyes light up. He takes my hand and leads me
    down a dark corridor, a bare hallway.

    He rests his hand on my shoulder.
    I rest my hand on his shoulder.

    He rubs my back—slowly,
    up and down. I rub his back.

    He turns and reaches his stubby arms around my neck,
    reaches up and kisses me again,

    before he ushers me out of the church, into
    the daylight, into the warm sunlit square outside.

*In the square, there are two churches, not just one—two
    great Baroque churches, facing each other—decaying,
    yet magnificent. Almost identical, except that one*

    is locked, and the door to the other is wide open."

Pornography

I. First Couple

On his knees, his back to us: the pale honeydew melons of his
        bare buttocks, the shapely, muscular hemispheres—

    the voluptuous center.

His knees push into the worn plush of a velvet cushion
        on the floral Oriental beside her cot.

He twists sideways—*contrapposto*—and bends to put his face
        into her crotch, between her limp legs,

    one hoisted by his right shoulder, the other—more
    like an arm—reaching around his back, her ankle
    resting on his naked hip.

    She's wearing shiny slippers with bows; he has on
    bedroom slippers and socks.

He's got a classic profile: straight nose, sharp chin.
        Cowlick. His hair tapers high on his neck,
        outlines his ear, in the current fashion;
                                her
    curly bob gives away the date (barely '20s).

His mouth grazes her private hair; lips apart, he
      keeps his tongue to himself.

He's serious: if he were wearing clothes, and she were something
      with pipes, he'd be a plumber's assistant—inspecting,
      studious, intent;
                            nothing erotic in his look, hardly
      aroused at all (a little hard to tell, of course,
      from behind).

Flat on her back, on the dark, fringed spread, gravity
      flattening her breasts, she looks

      uncomfortable, but not unhappy. Her eyes
      check out the camera. Her lips are sealed, yet—

      isn't there?—a trace of smile
      playing around the edges . . .

She stretches out an arm to him, places her palm
      flat on his head—guiding him so lightly, she

      might be blessing him.

II. Second Couple: The Sailor and His Girl

They're hot, half-dressed (upper half only), and they
      can't wait.

      He sports a sailor's midi and a mariner's
      beret (is that a mound of fishing nets
      she's lying back on?)
                        He rests his naked knee
      beside her ample thigh.

Her dress is long—Victorian and striped. If she hadn't
        raised it to her chest, it would be hiding her
        black knee-length stockings and black, mannish shoes.
        (He's also wearing shoes. How did he get his
        pants off?)
                No underwear—
                                nothing fallen around her ankles
        to keep her from spreading her legs.

Not quite supine, she strains forward to eye, and
        hold, his bold erection:
                                bat and hardballs—
        major league (his Fenway Frank; his juicy
        all-day-sucker).

He looks down hungrily at her hungry eyes
        and mouth—one hand pressed flush against
        his own naked thigh.
                        He slouches a little (not all of him is
        standing at attention), to make what she wants
        easier for her to reach.

But the photographer is sharp—he keeps his sharpest focus
        on what he's sure we want it on: all the

        fleshy folds, clefts, crevices—the no-longer-
        secret places—of her welcoming flesh.

He knows the costumes negate the spiritual burden
        (and freedom) of pure nakedness—
                                put us *in*
        medias res (things happening, things about
        to happen); in

on the guilty secret, complicit—one eye
furtively glancing over a shoulder . . .

His models rivet their attention on each other (did he
have to tell them?), so that we can be

riveted too.

Of course, they're only posing—
but despite the props and costumes, certain

undeniable details
suggest that it isn't—it

can't be—all an act.

III. *Ménage à Trois*

It's the heavy one—the one with the little pot belly, sagging
breasts, and double chin (practically all we can
see of her face)—that he's kissing so passionately.

Yet his arms are around them both, he loves them both
(and of course he couldn't kiss them
both at the same time).

Naked except for (like them) shoes and stockings, and garters,
he sits at the edge of an overstuffed easy chair,
his knees spread wide,
his massive cock
rising like the Leaning Tower from his gut.
His chest and neck, calves and thighs, have an athlete's
sculptured musculature:

exercise keeps all his parts in shape.

Both women are on their knees. She—the heavy one on his
        left (*our* right)—pushes into him, her round belly
        against his knee, her plush, round bottom
        a luxurious counterweight.

        Her fingers clutch his engorged organ, hang
        on to it, almost to steady herself.

The other one is slimmer, prettier, she has a pretty
        mouth—a delicate movie-star face.

        She's almost crouching, practically sitting on her
        own high heels; her right hand tenderly envelopes
        his testicles.
                        Hard to tell if she's smiling
        up at his face or down at his genitals—probably
        both, in equal admiration, adoration, desire.

His own benign, blissed-out look is
        harder to read, his shadowy profile
        half-buried in the intense kiss.

There's something sweet, *humane,* about them all: not
        innocent—
                        but nothing (well, almost nothing) hard,
        or hardened yet.

        Only the little they have on reminds us how
        openly this was intended to be obscene.

The composition itself is elegant—balanced, symmetrical:
        the sweeping curve of the pretty one's behind
        and back, flowing up and across the curve of the
        man's shoulders and neck,
                        then down again through the
        fuller arcs of the plump one's back and rump—

a harmonious circle of arms: theirs behind his back
supporting him; his around them—his hands resting
on their shoulders; their hands meeting in his lap . . .

It's like some medieval *Descent from the Cross* or *Holy
Burial:* the slumping Christ between two
ministering Angels—
                                    but inside out, inverted, a negative
of the Passion. Passion here only—and nothing
but—passion. Perhaps

not even passion.

This ancient postcard: cracked; corners broken; edges
frayed; worn and fragile

from use.

How many has it gratified; disappointed;
hurt? In whose horny fingers has it

been gripped (and did that hand
know what the other was doing)?

Not innocent—

but nothing about them
hard, or hardened yet;

not yet past taking pleasure
in whatever pleasure they

receive, or give.

Proverbs from Purgatory

It was déjà vu all over again.

I know this town like the back of my head.

People who live in glass houses are worth two in the bush.

One hand scratches the other.

A friend in need is worth two in the bush.

A bird in the hand makes waste.

Life isn't all it's crapped up to be.

It's like finding a needle in the eye of the beholder.

It's like killing one bird with two stones.

My motto in life has always been: *Get It Over With.*

Two heads are better than none.

A rolling stone deserves another.

All things wait for those who come.

A friend in need deserves another.

I'd trust him as long as I could throw him.

He smokes like a fish.

He's just a chip off the old tooth.

I'll have him eating out of my lap.

A friend in need opens a can of worms.

Too many cooks spoil the child.

An ill wind keeps the doctor away.

The wolf at the door keeps the doctor away.

People who live in glass houses keep the doctor away.

A friend in need shouldn't throw stones.

A friend in need washes the other.

A friend in need keeps the doctor away.

A stitch in time is only skin deep.

A verbal agreement isn't worth the paper it's written on.

A cat may look like a king.

Know which side of the bed your butter is on.

Nothing is cut and dried in stone.

You can eat more flies with honey than with vinegar.

Don't let the cat out of the barn.

Let's burn that bridge when we get to it.

When you come to a fork in the road, take it.

Don't cross your chickens before they hatch.

DO NOT READ THIS SIGN.

Throw discretion to the wolves.

After the twig is bent, the barn door is locked.

After the barn door is locked, you can come in out of the rain.

A friend in need locks the barn door.

There's no fool like a friend in need.

We've passed a lot of water since then.

At least we got home in two pieces.

All's well that ends.

It ain't over till it's over.

There's always one step further down you can go.

It's a milestone hanging around my neck.

Include me out.

It was déjà vu all over again.

The Dream During My Mother's Recuperation

At 89, my mother is in the hospital, mysteriously losing blood, when suddenly her stomach hemorrhages. She's rushed into surgery but is not expected to survive. Two years earlier, the hospital cardiologist prevented the operation that might have prevented this emergency: he thought her heart couldn't take it. After the operation, she remains in intensive care for three weeks, most of that time with a breathing tube down her throat so that she can't speak at all, though she can write short, very shaky notes:

TAKE IT OUT   thirsty   put my teeth in my mouth

I'll be here alone

Slowly, to everyone's astonishment, her strength begins to return.

These are some of the things she said to me in the hospital and, later, in the convalescent home:

"Worried about me?"

"It's a tough apple to chew on."

"I'm not doing anything, but I'm doing it the hard way."

"I might as well make a good job as none at all."

"I'm a human being. WORRY is one of my stations."

"I'm a specimen of deliberation."

"I'll sleep my years away."

"I'll let things go the way they come."

"I feel lost. I'm heading for nowhere. I have to stop somewhere to see where I'm landing."

"Whatever is going on will be going on without me."

"It passes so fast. That's life."

"The winter sun is like a stepmother's love."

"I'm one day closer to the end."

"Nothing goes easy for me."

"I can't stuff myself like a turkey."

"Sometimes I wake up and I don't know where I am. Then my mind begins to unravel, and I know where I am. Then there's some distraction, and my thoughts go behind bars."

"I'm not very happy here: people are so snobby, some of them think themselves more than they are. However, I don't give a hoot."

"I don't know what I'm doing. I'm on this side of the wall; I'm on the other side of the wall. I don't know what they want from me."

"I know the feeling, it's staring me in the face. I just can't throw it away."

"Did I just say something stupid?"

"The Cherinskys have been bubbling up in my mind."

"It's good to talk to you, you're giving me a line to live on."

"I'm OK. I'm not a world's winner, but I'm doing OK."

"Well, your mother came back."

"I'm whole again."

"I'm glad I'm not a question mark. I'm a human being."

"A lot of it was you pulling me back into a land of freedom, goodness, and love."

During the later stages of her recuperation, I dream we're about to embark on a long ocean voyage. The moment we board the ship, we're ordered to put on life jackets, or we will not be permitted to continue. Only my mother doesn't have one. I look everywhere. I comb every inch of the ship. I can't find one for her.

"I have so much to look forward to. I'm renewing my life all over again."

"What you hear from me, this is me."

"Let's live and tell these little stories."

No Orpheus

When he sang of what had passed, the trees would lean toward him, he could suspend the suffering of the damned, he could bring back the dead.

Don't look back! . . .

Hell is a spotless room
overlooking the ocean; she

wants out.

"I'm heading for nowhere, what do I have
to look forward to?"

She used to have
a future—

and a past. "I'm lost, I'm like
a stranger to myself."

"I'm an
unstationary pedestal."

"My marbles are slowly rolling away."

She's thrown out family
photos; no longer recalls

her husband, or her
maiden name. Still, she wants him

to lead her back.

"When am I going to see you?
Are we a long distance apart from one another?"

He wants her back.

He wants her back . . .

If it took only
not looking back

to lead her back, it would be easy
not to look, not to look

back; but if helping her look
back is the one way he knows to

help her back, then he has to help her
look back.

Where else could she look?

"I'll try not to remember
too many things. I'll just remember

what I can . . ."

Do we—don't we—have more
(he wishes he knew)

than what we look back to?

Her Waltz

"This is my dream. I'm dancing!
(Do you know how to dance? Do you
like to dance?) *Waltzing*—
it's like electricity.

It hurts when I walk. So I pick up a chair,
and I start to waltz.
I look in the mirror and there I am,
dancing with a chair!

I say to the mirror: 'I'm not so old.'
But the mirror says: 'Yes you are.
You're old. You're nearly
ninety years old. What are you doing

waltzing around with a chair?'
Now isn't that silly? An old lady.
This is my dream: I see myself in the mirror
waltzing with a chair.

And that's the end of my dream.
I once knew how to dance. I
once knew how to waltz.
And now I shall bid you goodnight."

Nostalgia (The Lake at Night)

The black water.

Lights dotting the entire perimeter.

Their shaky reflections.

The dark tree line.

The plap-plapping of water around the pier.

Creaking boats.

The creaking pier.

Voices in conversation, in discussion—two men, adults—serious inflections (the words themselves just out of reach).

A rusty screen-door spring, then the door swinging shut.

Footsteps on a porch, the scrape of a wooden chair.

Footsteps shuffling through sand, animated youthful voices *(how many?)*—distinct, disappearing.

A sudden guffaw; some giggles; a woman's—no, a young girl's—sarcastic reply; someone's assertion; a high-pitched male cackle.

Somewhere else a child laughing.

Bug-zappers.

Tires whirring along a pavement . . . not stopping . . . receding.

Shadows from passing headlights.

A cat's eyes caught in a headlight.

No moon.

Connect-the-dot constellations filling the black sky—the ladle of the Big Dipper not quite directly overhead.

The radio tower across the lake, signaling.

Muffled quacking near the shore; a frog belching; crickets, cicadas, katydids, etc.—their relentless sexual messages.

A sudden gust of wind.

Branches brushing against each other—pine, beech.

A fiberglass hull tapping against the dock.

A sudden chill.

The smell of smoke, woodstove fires.

A light going out.

A dog barking; then more barking from another part of the lake.

A burst of quiet laughter.

Someone in the distance calling someone too loud.

Steps on a creaking porch.

A screen-door spring, the door banging shut.

Another light going out (you must have just undressed for bed).

My bare feet on the splintery pier turning away from the water.

Song

rain on the lake
room at the lodge
alone in a room
in the lazy light

loons on the lake
geese in the air
moose in the woods
aware   awake

a cry dislodged
from the musty woods
the gamy musk
of the one aroused

the roaming moose
the rooms lit up
the woods awake
in the loony light

the moon dislodged
the lake aflame
the Muse amazed
amused   aroused

Renato's Dream

Brazil, 1991

Such a sweet dream. I dreamed
I was having a conversation
with the great poets—Manuel
Bandeira and Carlos Drummond
de Andrade. "I was born
tired, hungry, and cold," I said.
And Drummond answered, "I too."

Cairo Traffic

When the dead are called to work in the fields of the next world, it's the Ushabtis ("Answerers")—tiny faience figurines like mummies—who will respond. Servants for the afterlife: seed packets slung over their left shoulders, both hands sticking out through the bandages ready to sow the seed. The name of the deceased inscribed in hieroglyphs . . .

SHINING FORTH

THE OSIRIS

THE SERVANT

AND SCRIBE

HORET-HA

Your gift to me—now my guide.

1. The Desert

This is what's left after everything else
has been worn away. Mountains and rock:

sandpapered, sand-*blasted,* scraped away
by wind and water, blown away to dust.

Mirages: hills like pyramids (the most
direct path to heaven), sphinx-shaped rocks

watching over these wasted places.

Everything else is in motion: the Western Desert
("Sahara") stretches, reaches, drifts,

extends (hardly just "lies") farther
than any Eye but One can see—

its sinister contours playing tricks
on every eye.

The ancient world was buried by the desert.
And preserved by the desert.

If anything else is left, it's
under all that sand,

or has become sand.

2. Why?

I never particularly wanted to visit the Middle East. The art didn't interest
me—antiquities elsewhere were much closer to the world of literature, archi-
tecture, and painting I love. The politics repelled me. Family and other pres-
sures *("You haven't been to Israel! Why not?")* have always pushed me in just the
opposite direction.

Then why, after more than 25 years away from Western Europe, the source of
my deepest beliefs in human possibility—why am I here, flying over a desert?

* * *

It'd been a hard year—I needed to get away as fast and as far as possible. How
long since either of us had taken a real vacation? You'd always wanted to see
Egypt, though I would have rather . . . But who hasn't had some secret ro-
mance about the Sahara, the Sphinx, the Serpent of the Nile? The very name
Cairo stirs up Hollywood visions. You see an ad . . .

But at short notice, the only way to Cairo is by way of Tel Aviv.

* * *

I'm still only absorbing, sorting out our adventures, not yet contemplating them. I've swum in the clean Mediterranean, waded to my waist in Galilean flotsam, floated in the Dead Sea (the mud, heat, and fetid stillness were your vision of Hell). We've climbed Mt. Sinai; "seen" Mary's house and Peter the Fisherman's; "visited" the Nativity and Crucifixion. Golgotha is now *inside* the Church of the Holy Sepulchre—you lit candles there in your parents' memory. In a crevice of the Wailing Wall, I left a prayer for the health of those I love.

On the Via Dolorosa, near where Jesus carrying the cross is said to have met Mary, a sign: 4TH STATION T-SHIRTS.

Outside the Church of the Annunciation, Nazareth's neo-Italian-Modern architectural horror (across the street from Mary's Well Souvenir Shop), a turbaned pitchman accosts our group: "Americans don't enjoy breakfast," he announces. "Stop and enjoy the Holy Land! . . . Genuine wooden camel— one buck."

* * *

Every inch is politicized. In the Old City, our Israeli guide keeps pointing out how much everything improved after Jerusalem was reunified; how the Jordanians destroyed the synagogues but the Jews, he says, never retaliated. "Look at the beautiful condition of that mosque!"

The Wailing Wall undoes me. I put on a paper yarmulke and join the men bowing and nodding in prayer. When I touch the wall, some deep Jungian response I'd never have predicted makes me weep. *Hear, oh Israel!* I walk through Yad Vashem in tears, surrounded—devastated—by images of the Holocaust. ("This is a sad place," a nine-year-old English boy in our group remarks.) An eternal flame burns in the middle of a wide, flat, gray space dotted with the names of the extermination camps. These are the ashes of martyred

Jews. Later I ask myself how they knew these were strictly Kosher ashes? How could anyone be sure no gypsy ashes, or homosexual ashes, were mixed in? Can this be a place of spirit when its main reason for existing is to justify the survival of the state?

And yet, what better reason for existing?

And who could pass through the gardens of the Righteous Gentiles—each tree and shrub planted in memory of the individuals, or groups, who risked their lives to save a Jew (or gypsy, or homosexual)—and not be stirred by the survival of the humane impulse in the face of malevolence still too over-whelming to take in?

In Eilat, we stroll the waterfront in the morning heat. Next week, right where we're standing, a Palestinian frogman will come out of the water and stab an Israeli soldier. On busy Ben Yehudah Street (pedestrians only) in Jerusalem's tourist zone, kids—boys barely out of their teens, civilians—cruise the cafés and bars with semi-automatic rifles strapped around their shoulders. Each person we ask has a different defensive explanation. One young waitress tells us: "Not everybody likes this."

One evening, flashing red lights—a police barricade in the center of the street. No one pays any attention. Outdoor cafés are still crowded. We ask an Arab rug vendor what's going on. "Deenameet!" he whispers, in a thick Semitic accent.

* * *

Why are we here? Even before we leave the States, my qualms are increasing and multiplying. El Al security gets pretty personal. Why have I waited so long to go to Israel? Why am I not staying longer? I don't speak Hebrew? Why not? I'm not visiting relatives? Why not? I'm going to Egypt? Why would a Jew want to go to Egypt?

As we approach the coast of Israel at the end of our all-night flight, you notice a fighter jet buzzing past us in the opposite direction. "It's our guardian," the man in front of us explains. Before we board the plane to Eilat (we're heading to the Sinai for our first night in the Middle East), the same security questions. And once again, they don't ask you—so blond and fair-skinned—why *you* haven't been to Israel before.

* * *

I've never seen so much desert. On the flight south, the wild, gray mountains of Jordan are outlined on the left; the barren Negev spreads out endlessly below . . .

Crossing the border into the Sinai, no longer verboten, is still full of irritations, incompetence. I'm forced to fill out my entry form twice, even though I've made no mistakes. The border guard, who must stamp thousands of visas a day, stamps mine in the wrong place. Stupid? Malicious?

"In Egypt," our Israeli travel agent warned us, "never stay in anything less than a 5-star hotel." Ours, just a few hundred yards over the border, at Taba, looks across the Gulf of Eilat (or Aqabba) to the purple-mountained panorama (a mirage?) of Jordan and Saudi Arabia. Three 5-star restaurants. Freshly landscaped grounds (construction still going on). It was built after the Six-Day War. When Israel returned the Sinai to Egypt, an effort was made to bend the new border around the hotel. It failed. The Egyptians, however, couldn't maintain it; Israeli and wealthy Arab vacationers stopped coming. Now Hilton is restoring it to its former glory as a tourist Mecca.

The gulf is warm and clear. On our evening walk, we see a large iridescent green fish swimming close to shore. Tomorrow we'll be picked up in a land cruiser and head down the coast then inland across the desert to St. Catherine's monastery. We'll sleep in a tent, and be awakened for a moonlight climb to the summit of Mt. Sinai. The agency calls this leg of the tour the "Sinai Blitz."

* * *

What am I looking for? An adventure, right? Not a pilgrimage. Even rough-ing-it, there's a kind of glamour. It'll make a good story. We'll remember shaking and wrenching our way across the Sinai at 80 kph in the back of the land cruiser. Our handsome, gap-toothed bedouin driver loves to race his friend in the next cruiser. Are they brothers? lovers? Men here are so affectionate. And reckless.

> "Watch out for that hill!"
> "You mean that *bump?*"

> "Watch out for that bump!"
> "*What* bump?"

At 2:30 A.M. we're roused from our comfortable green and purple tents in the back courtyard of the St. Catherine hostel. We're poured coffee and handed plastic bags with hard-boiled eggs, wedges of processed cheese, and pita bread— our breakfast at the summit of Gebel Musa, the Mount of Moses. In the moonlight, you can make out only a crowd of outcroppings, sudden jagged silhouettes against the moonlight, and the all-enveloping desert. We're on the moon.

A millennium ago, monks cut 3,750 knee-breaking stone steps from the mountain. We choose the camel path. At the base of the summit, there'll be 750 more steps to the top. They worry you. Against the protests of Judah, our athletic, ascetic, intimidating guide (*me* he's got completely cowed), you hail a camel, which as you mount lurches you over the edge of the cliff. "Don't worry," the camel driver reassures, "camel never fall off mountain!"

I'm ahead of you for a while. Then you come trotting past me. My climbing partner is a 60-year-old Swiss farmer woman who, as the incline steepens, tells me her story, how when her husband died, her children inherited the farm and took it away from her. (Two hours later, when we reach the base of the summit, she leaves me breathless in the dust as she starts up the final 750 steps two at a time.)

At the top it's cold and crowded: candlelight ceremonies, Bible-readings, hymn-sings—in English, German, and Japanese. The rising sun lights up one craggy wave of peaks after another, each wave casting its shadow across the next. But it's impossible to extricate the sublime from the banal. Everything's for sale: campsites; postcards; chunks of local quartz and dendrite. "Cafeterias" (little tar-paper shacks) serve watery coffee, very hot chocolate (not bad!), and plain boiling water. Camel drivers hawk their assistance to footsore pilgrims.

Judah challenges us to take the steps all the way down for the more spectacular view, but you refuse (and insist I stay with you). The rocky descent is barely easier than the climb. You take the same camel and discover that riding downhill is especially problematic if you're male. You're in continual agony and have to stop often to "readjust." My feet hurt; I limp along beside you. But for the first time we can really see the mountain itself: a massive pipe organ carved out of bare rock—not the tallest peak in this congested range yet the one that looks most like the place where a God would deliver his Commandments to a Moses.

(Is there a difference between a *spiritual* and an *aesthetic* high?)

3. The Monastery

Behind red granite walls just above the foot
of the mountain, Saint Catherine's jeweled hand

and severed head are on view only to Holy People.
Tourists pump water from Moses's Well;

struck matches glint from gilded icons
that freckle the dim narthex. A thick

shrub overhangs a little shelf of rock
above a narrow courtyard: *the* Burning Bush!

—its leaves still green but dry
and rust-stained; you'd never guess.

The great library is off limits. *Thank
you, Konstantin von Tischendorf!* (In 1859, this famed

Leipzig Bible scholar wormed
the Codex Sinaiticus—one of our two oldest New

Testaments in the original Greek—
out of the monastery and into the treasury

of Czar Alexander. After the Revolution
the strapped Soviets sold it for a fortune

to the British Museum, which evidently
still feels no obligation to return it.)

In the charnel house, skulls are piled
in a caged cell—the remains of every monk

who's ever lived here; for centuries, each
one cooking his own meals.

They've never liked visitors: St. Stephen
himself, at a gateway high up the mountain,

used to sit in judgment
on who should be permitted to ascend.

Now his skeleton, still sitting (though much
better dressed—sporting a jaunty

violet "skull-cap"), keeps watch
over all the other bones.

4. *The River*

I'm all turned around. We're sailing *up* the Nile—i.e., south. West is on our
right (tombs are always on the western side).

Green plants rush past, roots and all. It's what they do. The current is swift;
the water is dark green. On the banks are farms and palms, adobe huts,
camels, wading water-buffalo. (We're in *Africa*.) The shore road is crowded
with donkey-carts to take us to the markets and temples. Behind the towns,
on either side, are nothing but dry brown mountains and sand. The river is
crowded with floating "hotels" (the M.S. Aida, the Nile Ritz, the Princess
Diana). Children in brown rags are in swimming—they stick close to the
banks. Efficient ferries dart between Luxor and the Valley of the Kings.

The air turns brown. A sudden sandstorm blows the desert into our mouths
and eyes. We have to move inside. Everyone's drinking—we're all thirsty all
at once.

There's too much food. Lunch today is roast turkey ("I picked it out myself
from the farm," the headwaiter tells me, winking, "—for you!") with cran-
berries and stuffing. The same two songs—"And I Love Her" and "Tara's
Theme"—are piped in over and over on the intercom. A young Carnaby
Street cockney couple, on their first international fling, are not at table. He's in
their cabin retching, the first to succumb to whatever it is we all eventually suc-
cumb to. You're next.

Two Genoese honeymoon couples are traveling with their entire families.
They have their own table and have little to do with us. On the quay at Esna,
brown-eyed little boys dance up and down near the passengers' windows and
with perfect accents are shouting:

"Come si chiama?" "Buon viaggio!" "*Pavarotti!*"

* * *

At Aswan, the first cataract, the old dam, and the new High Dam (the longest—not the highest—pile of stones and sand and concrete in the world) block our way; we can't sail any further. The new dam has increased irrigation and electric power, flooded temples, stopped the natural flow of silt, and transformed the great river into Lake Nasser ("the world's second largest artificial lake: 317 miles long").

Little motor launches taxi back and forth to the island-temples of Philae. High-sailed feluccas glide past the lush gardens of Kitchener's Island, the Cataract Hotel *(Death on the Nile),* the elephant-hide rocks of Elephantine, the stone steps on the bank that lead down to the Nilometer ("an ancient well marked to measure the water level and predict the extent of the annual inundation for the purpose of irrigation and taxation"), the spartan villa and mausoleum of the Aga Khan—until the wind dies.

On the western bank: a hill of burial grounds, a mosque in silhouette. We watch from the boat rail. Sunset slowly changes the color of the river. The water's burning. Everything's turning gold and violet.

* * *

In Cairo, our hotel (the Ramses Hilton) is right on the river bank. The river is wider than any street. Islands multiply the number of its branches, its many embracing arms. Across the river is the embroidered shaft of the Cairo Tower; beyond that the pyramids. The river once flowed right past them.

5. Cairo Traffic

The most dangerous place in the Middle East . . . especially if you want to cross the street. Our hotel is just across the square from the Egyptian Museum, but it takes half an hour to negotiate. No stoplights: cars just keep zooming at you.

"Find a pregnant woman," an experienced pedestrian advises, "it's the only way to be sure you won't be hit."

On the way in from the airport, traffic is mega-snarled. Cairo has just lost to Giza in the football game and a riot has broken out. Our taxi, so small I can't sit up straight in the back seat, worms its way through six and seven lanes of traffic on a three-lane road (drivers here have no concept of "the lane").

Cairo is a 24-hour horn fugue: Be-beep! *Be-beep!* Be-beep! *Be-beep!* Be-beep! *Be-beep!* No anger. No aggression. Just thousands of sweet little blurts, an-nouncements, self-proclamations: Here I come! Here I am! Watch out! Watch *me!*

We get a flat. But our ancient driver refuses our help as oncoming cars skirt us by inches. He's never heard the English for "flat tire," which delights him. As we wend and wobble our way into the city (the spare wasn't exactly full), we pass our pretty flight attendant in her stalled, overheated car. She displays an equanimity we don't share.

* * *

At Saqqara, I mount a camel behind Gomar Asmin. I'm uncertain about hold-ing onto his hips, and try to keep my balance as we sway. We canter in a wide circle around King Zoser's great Step Pyramid ("the oldest stone structure in Egypt, built by Imhotep"). We pass other pyramids: *Bent, Collapsed, Unfin-ished*—failed experiments, some just mounds of rubble.

Surrealist landscape. Shimmering on the horizon across the pink desert, in a military zone strictly off limits, more pyramids appear—one of them as grand and shining as Cheops's (maybe his father's). Gomar is talking about my brother. "Your brother," he says, "wants to go to America." But I'm an only child. It soon dawns on me that Gomar's English is as shaky as his camel. I try to correct him. I point to myself and say: "*My* brother." He nods and points to himself: "Your brother."

Before the ride is over, Gomar slides off and hands me the reins. He's letting me "drive" the camel myself! Off I gallop. Though the fee was negotiated beforehand, I give Gomar a much bigger tip than I had planned.

Palms line the farm road from the temple grounds. Saqqara is sleepy, clean—a rug-making center. We pass the Cleopatra Carpet School as we drive out of town.

* * *

In the dark rooms and dingy passageways of the Egyptian Museum, amidst the colossal kings of the "Smiling Period," sits solemn King Zoser, one arm locked across his chest. And stone-faced Chephren, the falcon Horus perched on the back of his throne, spreading its protecting wings around the pharaoh's neck. Tutankhamen, wide-eyed, golden, terminally ill (or poisoned) at nineteen. Akhnaten's wide hips and sensuous lips; his beauteous Nefertiti's pale unfinished head—more austere than the famous bust now in Berlin, yet still glamorous, knowing, even without eyes. A squatting scribe: legs crossed, a papyrus scroll spread across his knees—alert, listening.

Loving couples: smiling husbands with arms around their wives' shoulders; wives with their arms encouragingly around their husbands' backs. The dwarf Seneb, head of the royal textile works, perched cross-legged on a high bench, his hands clasped; his wife sits beside him—her feet touching the ground, her hand touching his arm. Prince Rahotep, High Priest of Heliopolis, with his sexy mustache; his black-haired wife, Nofret, positively gleaming in a transparent white limestone shift that barely conceals her small limestone nipples.

Upstairs, crowds gawk awestruck at the sumptuous array of King Tut's gold—rooms cluttered, hallways lined with it. Just around the corner reposes the three-thousand-year-old body of Ramses (but the royal mummy rooms are closed for renovation).

While you study the ancient coins, I go exploring. Is that seedy-looking guard watching me? He waits in the dusty corridor while I check out each deserted room. He follows me into one, slouches against a shadowy corner, and seems eager to show me something I'd be unlikely to find in the catalogue.

* * *

"Hey, Mustache! Nice mustache! . . . American? English?" At Luxor, up on the quay, young men call to us as we walk into town. "Want girl? Want boy?" All we want is a ride to the museum. "Taxi? I take you. Stay as long as you want. I wait."

At Karnak, I wander off alone, and come upon a fresh excavation. A police guard strides rapidly toward me. I back away—this dig must not be open to the public. He approaches faster; I retreat more quickly. Have I broken the law? I make my escape behind a row of columns. Later, I realize what he wanted. Our "Rhodesian" couple (their adjective) return to the boat in triumph. One of the lurking figures at Karnak has directed them—for a small fee—to some pornographic wall-carvings, which they now have on videotape. We all line up for a peek.

From the ramparts at Edfu, thin, nightgowned little boys toss tin cans on strings down to the tourists: our only actual "beggars"—everyone else offers something in exchange.

At Esna, we take a donkey-carriage from the great temple back to the dock. The back of the seat is pasted with glamour photos of Egyptian starlets. The driver wants a young English girl in our group to sit next to him: he hands her the whip. We pass a woman swinging a bunch of live pigeons by the feet. In Cairo, at a local "ethnic" restaurant, we order grilled pigeon ($3.50). It's so tasty, we ask the waiter for another portion. He brings two. We apologize, but we ordered only one. He's crestfallen. As we eat, he keeps passing our table with the extra plate of pigeon. Later, we think how little it would have meant to us to accept it.

6. Pyramids

The world is a pyramid.

They look just like the postcards, yet they're not exactly what I expected. The scale is bewildering. Is this a gigantic stage set, or a miniature? The Great Pyramid, first of the Seven Wonders (and the only one left), is taller than the Statue of Liberty, than St. Peter's (their relative heights are pictured in the guide book). Yet, its tip lopped-off, it looks shorter than the middle one, which is on a hill—a deliberate deception? First all three seem to overlap; then gradually they spread out along the winding road across the Giza plateau and into the Western Desert. There they are in the middle of nowhere, and right across the street from downtown. *(Is it all done with mirrors? Where am I?)* Drive down busy, dirty, divided Shari el-Haram ("the Road to the Pyramids"), the Main Street of Giza with its island of ragged palms, and see them rising—*looming*—over the high-rises, shadows on the hazy sky. What the photos can't convey is the staggering breadth: the perfect squares spread over acres. The Great Pyramid alone is more than half a mile around.

Perspective, proportion, symmetry . . .

> *Step right up! Get your ticket at the kiosk! Enter*
> *the sacred ancient City of the Dead!*

* * *

"Climb to top? Only half an hour." The sparse-toothed, blue-burnoosed Arab, eager for the meagerest baksheesh, tries to get us to make the same ascent the spirits of the dead kings were said to have attempted from within—before grave robbers descended to deny them their last shot at immortality.

On the desert side, a bedouin camp: tents, horses, cool camels, panting dogs lolling in any available shade. "Camel ride? Take your photo with the pyramids!" (He pronounces it "byramids.") "You have American cash? Ten

dollars, twenty dollars—pay what you like, pay later . . . You like my camel?"
The camel grins. His name is Michael Jordan.

* * *

"Do you wish to go in?" Our private guide asks politely, dubious, but willing
to wait. "Really, there's nothing inside." But I want to be alone in the sanctum
sanctorum. At the doorway, yet another guide is ready to tell us what we al-
ready know. He precedes us, unasked, lighting our way down the ribbed
gangplank of a three-foot-high shaft tilted 45 degrees. At bottom, we can
stand up straight, then have to crouch again for the 45-degree ascent to the
empty but airy interior.

Empty except for—"Oh, no!" (*I* am *not* polite)—two Americans from the
boat: retired bill-collectors from Chicago very much on the prowl, one a wid-
ower, the other divorced (easy to tell which is which); I thought we'd finally
ditched them. "Watch your head! Don't stand up! Gee, it's filthy. How'd you
like to get a girl in here?"

Near the foot of the Great Pyramid, we're welcomed into the new house of the
Great Solar Barque (or funeral boat) of Cheops—a Viking ship as long as a
tennis court, with a giant's oars—reconstructed from a thousand votive pieces
of sycamore and cedar. Just outside, more boats still lie buried, but there are
no funds for another resurrection.

* * *

We lunch at the Mena House Hotel, across the street. Where Churchill and Roo-
sevelt stayed, our guide dutifully informs us—and must have gaped at Khufu's
great graveyard through the same beaded curtains, out the same high windows.

We go to even greater lengths—to see them from every side and angle: from
our hired car; from miles away on the other side of the desert; from across the
city. We're obsessed (who isn't?). We envy fellow tourists whose arriving
planes have flown directly overhead (ours flew over Saqqara). They rub it in
(so would we).

Our last night, someone tells us we can see them from the balcony of our hotel room! I'd tried and failed when we first arrived. I was probably looking in the wrong direction. Or there was just too much haze. Tonight it's too dark to see anything. In the morning it's hazy again.

But just before we leave, they seem to . . . materialize. There, in the distance, just to the left of that modern tower! Three specks (the shape is unmistakable) just beyond the edge of the city. They hover above the horizon like tiny pointed angels—pointing the way to heaven?—which have just begun their departure from this world (itself a pyramid according to ancient lore).

7. *Sphinxy*

"Our Sphinx is sick."

A limestone scarf wraps your sore throat; a blanket
of white bricks covers your flanks. Dynasties

of changing weather (shifting winds, and a dampness
the Pharaohs never had to worry about)

have taken their terrible tolls, quite eroding
your health. The new government has you quarantined;

wants to evict the people across the street and cut off
their corrosive underground pipelines.

But mysterious Sphinx, delicate Sphinx—dwarfed
by the gigantic, indifferent monuments you're guarding,

four thousand years up to your neck in sand—
you're indifferent too.

Chephren's battered face, like a woman's (suffering,
impassive after centuries of mutilation), is still

alluring; your worn smile—worn *away*—is gentle,
ironic, despite your imposing lion length, and claws.

Our guide tells us there were "periods of
Smiling Faces"; later there'd be more

serious faces—however you God-Kings
wished yourselves perceived, and what was "in."

I want to rub myself up against your rump; pet
your paws; have my picture taken with you.

But you're unapproachable, practically the only
fenced-off monument in all of Egypt. Other sphinxes

one can still be intimate with: the white-faced
alabaster lion of Memphis; the grim phalanx

of Amon-Ra's ram's-heads at Karnak; the long-perspective
avenue of welcoming sphinxes

facing the pylon and two colossi of Ramses
at Luxor; even in the Museum, the pieced-together,

bearded-yet-feminine sphinx of the Pharaoh-Queen
Hatshepsut, the lion-woman whose nephew/stepson husband

tried to have every image of her defaced (Egyptians
weren't always high on family loyalty—think of Cleopatra

and her consort/kid-brother). We can look them all
right in the eye. But you remain aloof.

Not that you too don't know what it's like to be
in the way: you started your life-in-the-desert

as a gigantic boulder, a massive stumbling block
in the construction of the City of the Dead.

"Do something with it," Chephren must have told his
hired grave-diggers, and they began chipping away.

You're less a statue than a tremendous bas relief, a
"sculptured mountain." Now wind, and sand,

and the relentless subterranean dampness,
have added their own knives, files, and chisels.

Still, your butchered, sunburnt face
stares into the rising sun-god's daily glare,

and smiles and smiles.

Dear Sphinxy, tell me the riddle about, you know,
Time and Power and Families—the one you think you

have the answer to. Tell me your answer!
No . . . don't.

8. Temples

Luxor. Karnak.
Esna. Edfu.
Kom Ombo.
Abu Simbel.

Our itinerary rolls off the tongue like a prayer.

To whom?

Deities whose names could be verses for skipping rope ("Isis, Horus, Hathor, Ptah"); slapstick comedians ("Min, Mut, and Nut"); vaudeville teams ("Ladies and Gentlemen, Seth and Thoth!").

Ramses' endless erections; the lost arks of the Ptolemies; the gods' menageries (crocodile mummies at Kom Ombo, the falcon courtyard at Edfu). We see them rising above the Nile, or over a Sacred Lake ("Lake of Creation"), reflected in the Sacred Lake.

In Memphis.
In Thebes.

A blur. A phantasmagoria. Walls and pylons incised with gods and kings—aroused and conquering; humbly anointed. Warriors and slaves, Hittites and Nubians. Piles of severed penises. Voluptuous nudes and sophisticated surgical equipment. Cow-headed goddesses and baby hippos.

Cartouche. Scarab. Ankh.

Colossi: crossed-arm God-Kings wielding flail and crook; wife and kids tucked tucked between their legs, barely approaching their knees. Obelisks hewn out of a single stone.

Cinemascope courtyards with dimly-lit chambers—the Holy of Holies (altars for human sacrifice, our guide thinks we think). Hypostyle ("hippo-style"?) halls of fat columns, rounded or ribbed, with flowered capitals (papyrus, lotus). Columns without an inch of empty space (the monumental corridors of Karnak; the delicate, human-scale avenue at Philae). Multi-perspective alleys, chiaroscuro mazes for priests and kings, labyrinths through which we now play hide-and-seek with eternity.

Wonders!

Ruins; fragments . . . "Modified" by the Romans; defaced by the Christians (faces literally "de-faced"); shelled by the Turks; toppled by earthquakes—or relatives. Vandalism. Terrorism. Crumbling buildings with traces of ancient paint. *"My name is Ozymandias, King of Kings . . ."*

Deep inside empty tombs, luminous images of the journey to the next world; blue ceilings (the night sky) swarming with little five-branched stick-figure stars, homunculi, each one a human soul.

9. So?

New York. Temple of Dendur, Metropolitan Museum of Art. In that giant temperature-controlled greenhouse on the edge of Central Park, such a tiny temple—prettier here than it ever was along the Nile? A gift to us in return for our contribution to the rescue of a greater temple from the flood created by "what must increasingly be regarded as an ecological, sociological, and economic disaster: the Aswan High Dam." I'd always loved it.

So barely back a minute, I go back to the Met, to this mini-temple, with its shallow artificial moat, photos on the wall of its original site and how it was saved, people milling, a guard standing by to make sure no one gets or tries to get inside—so that it won't lose a millimeter, a milligram of dust. Our passion to preserve is practically a religion. We want the Temple of Dendur to last for-ever. And who am I, materialist that I am, to object?

For the first time, everything in the Egyptian wing makes sense—the statues, the mummy-cloths, even the maps now have a context.

But something else has happened.

No, I haven't converted, though in fact I find I have a lot of sympathy with el-ements of what I understand to be the religion of Ancient Egypt. Life and Death, Order and Chaos seem to have been worshipped equally; and I, who believe there's a reason for everything, that everything makes sense if one tries hard enough—I believe with equal conviction that reason is an illusion, that nothing *ever* makes sense. I'm afraid I'll lose the past, so I don't throw anything away; so I live in chaos. A visitor once asked if I was planning to take every-thing with me to the next world.

My real conversion took place when I was thirteen: I lost confidence in religion (I still believed in morality). Later, I believed in art. In Israel, at the Western Wall, I found a surprising residue of feeling for everything I'd been taught to worship as a child.

But in Egypt, something else—something about the relation between how massive these monuments are, how heroic, and how old (older than almost anything else we call art) and fragile. They've been on earth so long, they seem tired of it—tired of time.

They're shrinking by the week, by the hour. On the river bank, at the edge of the mountains and the desert, we tromp over stones and dirt (there's still some sand in my shoes), we lean on columns, pet the sphinxes, rub the giant scarab for luck. They don't resist—they've never resisted—the daily inva-sion of priests and pilgrims, guards and guides, postcard-sellers and photo-opportunists, righteous gentiles and holocaust victims; each of us taking our little souvenir as we pass through.

They don't look down. Above our human heads, the temples, or what's left of them, are moving into their other life. You can practically hear them slipping away, following those who built them (stumbling over stones, sand in their shoes) and those who had them built: their dust returning eagerly to dust.

Is this the body through which the spirit breathes? My brief Egypt! Graphic close-up of my own dissolution. In this carnival of souls, half marketplace, half theater, in this un-holy land where the spirit sleeps and nothing is not for sale, the spirit wakes, struggling to remain in this world while the beautiful body falls away.